Secrets of Traveling on Social Security

How to Get Transportation, Accommodation, and Meals Dirt-Cheap or Free

Jerry Minchey

www.LifeRV.com

Stony River Media

ISBN-978-0-9905945-5-0

1. Budget Travel

2. Solo Travel Guides

3. Budget Travel Guides

Published by Stony River Media

Knoxville, Tennessee

StonyRiverMedia.com

Disclaimer

The information in this book is based on the author's knowledge, experience, and opinions. The methods described in this book are not intended to be a definitive set of instructions. You may discover other methods to accomplish the same end result. Your results may differ.

There are no representations or warranties, express or implied, about the completeness, accuracy or reliability of the information, products, services, or related materials contained in this book. The information is provided "as is," to be used at your own risk.

This book is not intended to give legal, financial, or medical advice and is sold with the understanding that the author is not engaged in rendering legal, accounting, medical, or other professional services or advice. If legal, financial, or medical advice or other expert assistance is required, the services of a competent professional should be sought to ensure you fully understand your obligations and risks.

All trademarks appearing in this book are the property of their respective owners.

There are several links provided to resources and companies in this book that I think might be helpful to you.

To be clear, I do not receive any commission or revenue from these links. They are just my recommendations for you to look at and decide if you think they would be helpful for your needs.

Version 2021.01

Table of Contents

Introduction

"You only live once, but if you do it right, once is enough."

~ Mae West

Today, there are so many ways to travel inexpensively (or even for free).

Now there's no reason why you can't be traveling.

I hear a lot of people say that they would love to travel if they could afford it.

In this book, I'll show you how you can travel cheaper than you can stay home.

This book will change your mind about traveling. It's not about theory, philosophy, or conventional wisdom. It's about the practical ways I travel in the US and all around the world while spending very little money.

Three parts of travel can be expensive

These three things are:

- Transportation

- Overnight accommodations
- Meals

If these three items in your travel budget were paid for or were free, I'm sure you could afford to travel on just your Social Security check with no problem.

In this book, I'll show you how these three budget items can be free part of the time and heavily discounted when they're not free.

This method of traveling is so much more enjoyable than going on a planned expedition that would cost you an arm and a leg. On top of that, a planned group trip probably wouldn't be enjoyable anyway. For sure, it wouldn't be enjoyable if you're a free spirit wanting to do and see things on your own and at your own pace.

To make inexpensive travel happen, here are some things you might have to do.

- Think outside the box.
- Carve your plans in Jell-O.
- Become more of a free spirit.
- Be a traveler and not a tourist.
- Be flexible.
- Don't get bent out of shape by changes.
- Travel with very little stuff.

An example of traveling light

A few months ago, I came back from a five-month trip to Costa Rica. All I carried with me was a small backpack and an even smaller carry-on bag.

I never wore most of the clothes I took with me. I could have traveled a lot lighter. While I was there, I only wore shorts and tee shirts.

I had three computers with me. One I was taking for a friend, and one was a backup.

The reason I carried a backup computer was that I didn't want to take a chance of my main computer dying or being stolen. Then I would be forced to pay an exorbitant price for one that didn't have the features I would want and need in a computer.

I also carried a small voltmeter (after all, I'm an engineer) and I also took a lot of video equipment and lights. (As usual, most of it I never used.)

Most people take way too much stuff when they travel. While they're packing, they say, "I might need this, or I might need that," and they take it.

Remember that, even in remote places, there will at least be a trading post. If you need anything, you can buy it.

I know one person who travels with a toothbrush, computer, cell phone, and one change of clothes.

When he gets to where he's going, $100 to $200 will buy all the clothes and other things he needs. When he's ready to leave, he donates everything to someone he's met or to a Goodwill type store.

Everything he travels with fits in his fanny pack—even his little computer.

Traveling light gives you a lot of freedom. We'll talk more about that later.

One final point: You can read this book straight through, from front to back, but you can also read the chapters out of order. You can pick out the chapters or topics that interest you and read those first.

In order to make each chapter stand alone, you will occasionally find that I have repeated a statement that was made in a previous chapter. Understand that there is a reason for this. The statement was needed in both places to cover the subject in that chapter.

Bottom line: Learn the techniques described in this book that I've used to travel dirt cheap while meeting people all over the world and having the time of my life. In this book, you'll learn how to travel free (or almost free) and on your terms. Why would you want to travel any other way?

Chapter 1

Life Is Short—and So Is Money

"You can be young without money, but you can't be old without it."

~ Tennessee Williams

You have to have a dream or you can't have a dream come true.

By having a dream, I don't mean a dream such as, "I want to retire and do some traveling sometime." I'm talking about what some people would call an unreal, crazy kind of dream—a dream that breathes new life into the dull routine of your day.

Do you want to live in a bungalow in the south of France, a cabin in the mountains, next to a beach, in a condo in the middle of downtown, on a farm, or, best of all, live in several different places and travel back and forth between them?

I can hear you now saying that all those things take money, but the truth is I'm almost sure you can live those lifestyles (and do a lot of traveling) for less than it costs you to live like you're living now.

When you get rid of your house and don't have any expenses back home while you're traveling, things get a lot easier.

If your dreams don't scare you, maybe they're not big enough.

A lot of people think of a dream as wishful thinking. For example, they dream of winning the lottery. But that kind of dream won't cut it. Your dream must be a burning desire that you're going to make happen come hell or high water, as the saying goes.

If you want to live a traveling lifestyle, you're going to have to change some things in your life.

I'm sure you don't want to change everything in your life. You probably want to keep your dog (and maybe your spouse), but you would like to change about everything else.

Don't wait for things to get easier, simpler, or better. Life will always be complicated. Learn to be happy right now. Otherwise, you'll run out of time. You will never have all the answers.

Start traveling before you're ready. Most people who travel say their only regret is that they didn't do it sooner.

Here are the secrets to low-cost traveling

The secrets to low-cost traveling fit into three categories.

1. **Reduce your average nightly accommodation expenses.** You can have some nights free, some low-cost nights, and splurge and spend a reasonable amount for other nights. The average is what's important.
2. **Cut your transportation expenses to the bone.** There are several ways to do this. The first and easiest way is to stay in one place longer. Don't travel every day. Maybe only travel once a month. When you travel every day or every few days, you miss out on experiencing the area you're visiting. Why go on to the next place when you haven't seen or experienced the area you're visiting? I'll talk about ways to travel inexpensively in a later chapter.
3. **Reduce your average food and daily expenses to a ridiculously low level.** The secret is not to eat out much, and when you do, don't go to chain restaurants or tourist restaurants.

Eating out should be considered a special occasion, but if you do it all the time, it's no longer special.

When you do eat out, eat at a local mom and pop cafe. They cost much less, have local food, have better food, and you will experience the local culture and atmosphere. (After all, that's the reason you're traveling in the first place.)

You could be living a life you don't need a vacation from.

One of the many things you'll love about the traveling lifestyle is that you'll usually be around people (old and young) who are making decisions and doing things. Your life will never be boring.

Hit the road and soak in whatever slice of the world you can. Breathe in deeply and experience the calm of the wilderness (a wilderness is anywhere that's new to you). Feel renewed and live a life with no stress. What are you waiting for?

Remember this:

"People don't take trips, trips take people."

~ John Steinbeck

Bottom line: Yeah, life is short, and so is money, but if you finish reading this book and use the techniques I describe, you'll find that you'll have plenty of money and time to travel. And all you'll need is the income from your Social Security.

Chapter 2

How Much Will You Receive from Social Security?

"Too many people are thinking of security instead of opportunity. They seem more afraid of life than death."

~ James F. Byrnes

Let's stop for a minute and see how much money you'll have to pay for your traveling adventures. Can you afford to travel if your Social Security income is all you have?

I'm not an accountant, and the following information should not be considered financial or tax advice. This is just my understanding of the laws and rules.

Reading about the rules and regulations concerning Social Security is about as boring as anything can get. I'm glad I'm not making my living as an accountant or financial adviser.

Be sure to check with your accountant or financial adviser for the latest laws and regulations.

I'll quickly get to the only thing you want to know, and that is how much your Social Security check will be.

There's a complicated formula to determine that, and we'll talk about it later. I assume that right now all you want to know is an approximate number. Here it is.

As of January 2021, the government reports that **the average person receiving a Social Security check will get 1,543 a month, and an average couple will get $2,596**.

You may receive more than this or less. That makes sense. That's why it's called an average.

This may be all you wanted to know, so you can skip the rest of this chapter and get on with learning how you can travel on this amount. It can be done quite easily.

If you want to know exactly how much you'll receive, keep reading.

If you're a glutton for punishment and want to know more about Social Security income numbers, keep reading this chapter.

If you're already receiving your Social Security payments, you know how much you're receiving each month. If that's the case, you probably skipped this chapter.

Do you even qualify to receive Social Security?

Getting the answer to whether you qualify to receive a monthly Social Security check is one of the few simple and straightforward answers in the Social Security rule book.

To receive a monthly Social Security check, you must have worked for at least 40 quarters during your lifetime (and earned $1,220 or more in each quarter—indexed to today's numbers).

By the way, if you worked ten years straight, that would be 40 quarters, but the ten years don't have to be consecutive.

Those 40 quarters have to be where Social Security Payroll taxes (also known as FICA) were deducted (or you reported and paid self-employment taxes).

Of course, you also have to be 62 years old before you can start receiving your benefits.

If you start drawing your Social Security benefits before reaching your full retirement age, your benefits will be less.

To find out exactly how much your Social Security benefits will be, you can either go to your local Social Security office (plan on being there for an hour or more) or you can go to the government website at https://www.ssa.gov/myaccount/ and go through the steps of setting up your account. This will only take a few minutes.

Your spouse (and/or ex-spouse) will be able to receive Social Security benefits, too, based on your work record. (When they receive benefits, it will not change how much you receive in any way.)

How is the amount of your Social Security payment calculated?

When you visit your local Social Security office or use the website linked to above, they have the records to calculate your payment amount, but here, in a nutshell, is how the amount is determined:

They take the payroll and self-employment income you earned each year you worked (up to what is call the "tax max," which was $142,800 in 2020 but of course was a lot less in previous years).

They take the amount you made (and paid Social Security on) each year, and then they index each year to account for inflation.

For example, if you made $25,000 in 1980, they would count it as $79,001 in today's dollars.

Then they take the 35 years with the highest indexed earnings and average these and then divide this number by 12 to determine your Average Indexed Monthly Earnings or AIME.

The government loves to use acronyms. The next two acronyms we'll talk about are PIA and FRA. PIA stands for your Primary Insurance Amount. That's the amount you will be eligible to receive when you reach Full Retirement Age, or FRA as they call it.

Below are the numbers showing what the Social Security Administration calls your FRA, or, in other words, the age when you can start drawing your full retirement amount.

When can you start drawing your full Social Security benefit?

You can start collecting Social Security at age 62, but at what age can you start drawing your full benefit? Here are the numbers.

If you were born between 1943 and 1954, your Full Retirement Age is 66. If you were born in 1955 or later, see the information below to see the age when you can start drawing your full retirement income:

1955 – 66 and 2 months

1957 – 66 and 4 months

1958 – 66 and 6 months

1958 – 66 and 8 months

1959 – 66 and 10 months

1960 and later – 67

Something to consider—The amount you will receive each month will continue to go up until you reach age 70. After that, it doesn't go up anymore, so by all means, apply and start receiving your payments no later than when you turn 70.

Here's one other point—To encourage you to continue working and paying into Social Security, your earnings are not indexed after age 60. What this means is that the money you make after age 60 will be worth more in calculating your Social Security payments.

Can I earn money and still draw Social Security?

In 2021, you can earn up to $18,960 without having it impact your Social Security benefits. If you've reached your Full Retirement age (FRA), there's no limit to how much you can make without it reducing your Social Security payment.

Your Social Security payment will be reduced by $1 for every $2 you make over $18,960. Note that investment and pension income doesn't count. It's only earned income that counts.

During the year you turn 66, your benefits will be reduced by $1 for every $3 you earn over $50,520 (for 2021) and only the months before you turn 66 will be counted.

You may have to pay income tax on your Social Security income

The rules are simple. If your income is less than $25,000, you don't have to pay tax on any of your Social Security income. If you make between $25,000 and $34,000, you have to pay tax on 50% of your earned income, and above $34,000, you have to pay income tax on 85% of your income. Note that only income that's earned is counted. Income from investments and pensions, etc. is not included.

You might say, "All of that's interesting, but I want to take what I can get now and start traveling. That's why I'm reading this book."

Bottom line: As was stated at the beginning of this chapter, the average person gets $1,543 a month from Social Security, and the average couple gets $2,596.

Unless you've gone through the steps and know what your Social Security income will be, keep those average numbers in mind as you go through the rest of this book, and let's see what you can do with that income. I think you'll be pleasantly surprised.

Chapter 3

Free and Low-Cost Accommodations and Meals

"The world is a book, and those who do not travel read only a page."

~ Saint Augustine

Keeping living expenses low is the key to low-cost travel.

Day-to-day living expenses when you're traveling can blow even a rich person's budget if you don't watch them. In this section, I'll be talking about only food and housing. I'll talk about transportation costs later.

You can't begin to do any low-cost traveling until you find a way to get your living expenses low while you're traveling.

There are a lot of ways to keep your living expenses low when you're traveling. Below is a brief description of some of the most common ways savvy travelers do it.

Free and low-cost accommodations

- **House-sitting.** This gives you free accommodations. One significant advantage of house-sitting is that it allows you to experience different living situations. If you've never tried it, how do you know you would like or not like living in a tiny house, living in a condo in the middle of downtown, living on a farm, etc.? You can use this website to find places you can stay. https://www.trustedhousesitters.com/. There's an annual fee of $129 a year to join.

- **Pet-sitting.** I have friends who do a lot of pet-sitting gigs. They go through the same website for pet sitting and for house sitting. https://www.trustedhousesitters.com/. There's an annual fee of $129 a year to join just like it is for house-sitting.

  They don't get paid, but they get to stay in some lovely houses (many times with swimming pools, hot tubs, etc.). They love animals, and they're traveling around the country in their van, so they apply for gigs in areas where they will be. The site allows the pet owner to leave feedback (kind of like eBay) on the pet-sitter or house-sitter. They have an excellent feedback score, so they pretty much get most of the gigs they apply for. They love animals and enjoy their adventures.

- **Swap your skills for accommodations.** I've done carpenter work, remodeling, painting, photography, and computer work (setting up websites, installing PayPal and other computer apps) in exchange for free or reduced-rate accommodations. I've stayed in beachside bungalows in Northern Australia and gone on safaris in India and Africa all in exchange for promoting the places in my books and on my websites.

- **Do you have a list?** Whether you have a YouTube channel, a blog, a Facebook group or a list of subscribers to your newsletter, if you have a list, it could be valuable when it comes to doing promotions in exchange for free accommodations. I've done it many times. Think about it. When owners or managers have unused facilities available in the off-season, it costs them almost nothing to give you free rooms. The key is that you have to ask and make them an offer they can't refuse. I've done it many times and I very seldom get turned down when I make the right offer.

- **Wwoof.net.** (This stands for **W**orld **W**ide **O**pportunities on **O**rganic **F**arms.) This website lists opportunities to live on organic farms. The arrangements vary, but generally you do volunteer work on an organic farm for 20 hours a week in exchange for free meals and accommodations. You usually sign up for 30 days at a time. I have never done this, but I know two people who did this. One worked on a horse farm in Tennessee, and one worked on a goat farm in Florida. They both thoroughly enjoyed the experience. In addition to taking care of the animals, they did some work in the garden. The farm grew a lot of their own organic vegetables. The work was not hard, and they met a lot of interesting people. These opportunities are available all over the US and in several foreign countries. There's a small fee ($40 for just the US with an additional cost to add other countries) to join and see all of the current listings. When you live for a month with absolutely zero living expenses, that gives you twice as much money the next month to spend on travel.

- There are other websites that offer accommodations and meals in exchange for a few hours of volunteer work. Here are some of them.

- **Helpx.net.** (The fee is $24 for a two-year membership.)
- **Workaway.info.** (The fee is $36 for an individual and $46 for a couple to join for a year.)
- **Peace Corps.** The Peace Corps provides each Volunteer with housing and a living stipend that enables them to live like people in their community of service. At the end of two years of service, you will receive $10,000. You don't hear as much about the Peace Corps as you used to, but it's still alive and well and a great way to experience living in another country. You can find out more about the Peace Corps at this link. https://www.peacecorps.gov/.
- **Couch surfing:** It's pretty much what the name implies. You can find out more about it at the link below:

  https://www.CouchSurfing.com/. You stay with a host for free and sleep on their couch or blow-up mattress (and yes, sometimes you get to sleep in a real bed in a guest room). You are essentially staying with a friend. You have friends all over the world. You just haven't met them yet. It's free to use the website, but there's a small fee to become a "verified" member. If you're going to be doing any couch surfing, I recommend that you get verified so the host can trust that you are who you say you are.

Like hostels, this technique tends to be used by younger folks, but you're young at heart. It's a great way to get to experience an area and get to know the locals. It's used a lot by people doing international travel.

- **Camping**. You'll have to spend a little money to get the necessary camping equipment if you don't already have it, but you can get everything you need at Goodwill or other such stores for very little money. Depending on where you camp, sometimes it's free, and sometimes you have to pay a small fee, but even if you pay a fee, it's way less than renting a room. There are tons of places all over the world where you can camp for free. You can find these places online by using this website.

  https://www.campendium.com/

  The website shows a lot of information about each location, including reviews and even the cell phone signal strength for the different carriers. There's a $20-a-year fee if you want to use all of the website features.

- **Backpacking and cycling**. This is a popular way to get to see and experience a country (or even a part of the US). I have a friend who has biked across the US from coast to coast. She also spent three months riding her bike all across Europe. Oh, the stories she can tell.

If you're going to do backpacking or cycling, I would suggest that you plan your trip to take advantage of seasons when the weather is mild. It takes a lot of the joy out of a trip if the weather is extremely hot or cold.

I've hiked through the jungles of Uganda and slept in a tent to see the silver-back gorillas. I've ridden elephants through the jungles of India to see tigers. (You don't want to be hiking looking for tigers. It's better to be sitting up on top of an elephant when you find a tiger.)

I've also been hiking and floating down rivers in China. I did all these adventures when the weather wasn't hot or cold. It made all the difference in the world.

Other low-cost ways to live while you're traveling

Until this point, I've mainly been talking about ways to get free rooms and meals, but sometimes you have to pay for accommodations. That's fine. You can splurge occasionally. It's your average cost per night that matters.

I've found that if you rent an apartment for a month at a time, you can get very reasonable prices anywhere in the world if you shop around.

In the last two years (before COVID), I've had friends use these techniques and they got great monthly prices for apartments in Spain, Italy, and Florida. I've used the techniques to rent nice apartments in Costa Rica for dirt-cheap rates.

For the ultimate low-cost accommodations, consider living in your car for a while.

There are dozens of YouTube videos showing how people live and sleep in their cars. It's not that they can't afford a different way of life; it's just a different experience and a different adventure. Watch some of these videos and see what you think before you dismiss the idea.

Find great deals through the grapevine

One of the best ways to find great deals on places to stay is to do it after you arrive. You can stay in an Air B&B or hostel for a night or two while you look around.

Most people want to have a place to stay nailed down, at least for a few nights, before they arrive in a new location. My son likes to fly into a country and find something after he gets there. He said, "I've never had to sleep on a park bench yet."

When you get to the city you want to stay in, check bulletin boards in coffee shops, ask people you meet if they know a good place to rent for a week or a month, talk to other people in cafes, etc. This technique will get you the best rates but get online and you can find some great rates and have less stress by knowing you have a place at a rate that fits your budget.

Also, check out Facebook groups for the cities that you're going to be visiting.

Whether you're driving to Kansas or flying to Rome, these techniques work the same worldwide.

How to keep your expenses down

Don't eat out much. Cook your own meals most of the time. When you do eat out, do **not** eat at chain or big-name restaurants. Eat at small mom and pop cafes. The food will be better, it will cost less, and you will experience more of the local atmosphere.

If you do want to splurge and eat out at a fancy restaurant now and then, go to www.Groupon.com and find a Groupon certificate for the restaurant you want to visit, and you could save up to 70% on a nice meal.

Be sure to read all of the fine print. Sometimes these are only good for certain days or may not include alcohol. This is a great way to save money **if** you actually use the coupon. A lot of people buy the coupons and then never use them.

Barter—the underused secret to low-cost travel

People who can be trusted and have skills are valuable and hard to find all over the world.

I'm sure you have more skills that are in demand than you realize.

For example, do you know how to defrag a hard drive on a computer? How about how to install Microsoft's free antivirus software or how to find and remove Malware from a computer?

Almost all computers will have some Malware. When you find this and show somebody how to remove the Malware, you will look like a hero.

If you don't know how to do some of these things, you can watch some YouTube videos and soon be an expert.

Almost everybody has a desire to write a book sometime. If you know even the basics of Photoshop, you can design a book cover for them. After they have a book cover designed, it's a lot easier for them to get motivated to start writing their book.

I've bartered for free or reduced-rate housing for years.

I've set up websites, incorporated PayPal on websites, done painting and carpentry work, and done yardwork. Some of the things I've done have been intellectual type work and some have been brute-force manual labor. That's fine. I always need the exercise.

I have friends who were staying at a B&B in Hawaii for two weeks. They got to be friends with the couple who owned the place. The couple was complaining that they never got a break. They had to work every day.

To make a long story short, my friends worked out a deal with the owners where my friends would come and run the B&B for two weeks every year in exchange for staying there for two additional weeks. They have been doing this for several years now. Everyone is happy.

Don't sell yourself short.

Bottom line: The world is full of free and low-cost accommodations. You just have to search for them and be creative. Make use of the websites and ideas that have been presented in this chapter, and you will be well on your way.

Chapter 4

How to Book Free and Cheap Flights

"The more I learn about people, the more I like my dog."

~ Mark Twain

I have flown over two million miles on Delta and a ton of miles on several other airlines. I've flown all over the world. I've been to every continent (except Antarctica).

I've used a lot of tips, tricks, and techniques to get the cheapest flights available. The rules change all the time, so what worked a few years ago may not work now or may not get you the absolute lowest price.

Note that some of the cheapest flights are not listed on many of the booking sites because the airlines don't pay the sites a commission (that's how they can offer cheaper fares).

This chapter covers the latest apps, tips, tricks, websites, and techniques for 2021 and shows you what works.

After a year of COVID-19, a lot of people are reluctant to fly. I think now being on an airplane is one of the safest places you can be. The air is filtered every few minutes through super fine filters. It's also been verified that the virus cannot be transferred by you touching surfaces. To be extra safe, all surfaces in airplanes are thoroughly cleaned between flights.

Of course, by all means, get vaccinated. Since I'm an old fart, maybe I can be in one of the first groups to qualify to get vaccinated—right after health care workers and nursing home residents. Don't let fear keep you from flying.

My seven techniques for booking cheap flights

A lot of people are looking for ways to fly as affordable as possible. The heck with affordable. When I take a trip, I want better than affordable. I want to fly cheap!

That's what I'm going to show you how to do in this chapter.

I always start my search by checking this website,

https://www.skyscanner.com

On this site, I can find the cheapest flights to where I want to go. Here I can check different days because it's cheaper to fly on some days. I've found that Tuesdays have the best fares many times but not always.

Do you remember the Huckleberry Finn story where Aunt Sarah was reading the Bible to him? She read all about the good place and then she started reading about the bad place. Old Huck said, "I wish I was there." Aunt Sarah got all mad. He said, "I didn't mean no harm. I just wanted to go somewhere."

If you're like Huckleberry Finn and you just want to go somewhere, and you don't really care where you go, check out the Google Flights website at the link below.

https://www.google.com/travel/explore

It shows you the fare from your home base to everywhere in the US, and then you can expand it to show you the fares to everywhere in the world.

You can click on the little calendar icon and find the cheapest flights for the next week, month, or even for the next year.

You might be surprised at how cheaply you can fly to a lot of places.

The day and time you fly can make a big difference. On Google Flights, you can click on the calendar icon and see the cost of flights on different days. Sometimes flying one day sooner or later can save you hundreds of dollars.

Be flexible with which airports you fly into and out of. Sometimes there's a big difference in fares.

The Google Flights website lets you enter up to five departure and five destination airports. Compare the fares and you may find that a little inconvenience might save you a lot of money.

Websites get sneaky

Sometimes when websites see that you've been searching for a flight over and over, they'll jack up the price of the flight.

Switching your browsing mode to private by going to the "New incognito window" and clearing your cookies can sometimes save you money. It's easy to do this in Google Chrome.

On the right side of the navigation bar at the top of the page, click on the circle that has three dots inside. In the drop-down menu that pops up, click on "New incognito window." You might be surprised at how many times these few keystrokes will save you money.

Here's how to get an extra 4% discount when booking your flights. Sign up with Ebates (it's free) and then go to Expedia to book your flight instead of going directly to the airline's website. They will show you the same price.

Ebates has a Google Chrome browser extension, so it will show up. Then you click, "Activate," and it applies your discount, and the money shows up in your bank account.

Volunteer to get bumped. Different airlines have different rules, and they change from time to time, but whatever the rules are at the time you get bumped, it's a good deal if you're flexible. I'm always flexible. I don't have to be anywhere at any certain time.

I've heard so-called travel experts say to wait and be the last person to check in and maybe you'll get bumped. I've managed to get bumped many times, and that's **not** the way to do it.

Get to the gate as soon as you can and when you check in, tell the gate agent you're willing to be bumped if the flight ends up being oversold. If it looks like the flight might be oversold, the agent will put your name on a list.

Wait patiently in the gate area, and if you're the first name on the list, you'll be the first person called if they need someone to volunteer to be bumped.

Sometimes the next flight is only an hour or so later, and sometimes it's the next day. You'll get from $200 up to $1,000, or a voucher for a free flight or whatever they're offering and be on the next flight to your destination.

If you have to stay overnight, you'll get a free room, and if you have to wait at the airport long, you'll get a free meal voucher.

The only disadvantage to volunteering is that if you don't end up getting bumped, you will be one of the last people to get on the plane and the overhead storage bins may be full. You might have to put your carry-on bag back in the back of the aircraft, or, even worse, you might have to have them check it for you. This doesn't happen often, but it does happen when the plane is full or almost full.

One more site to check

Most of the websites helping you find cheap airfares make their money by receiving commission from the airlines when you book your flight.

Some of the cheapest flights are on airlines that don't pay these commissions, and because of that, some of the major flight booking websites don't show their flights.

http://Matrix.itaSoftware.com is a website that doesn't get commissions from the airlines (maybe because you can't actually book a flight with them) but you can find cheap fares on this site.

Check them out before you book your flight and see if you can find a better price than you've found using the previous sites I've mentioned.

You can't book your flight using this site, but after you find the flight you want, go directly to Google Flights or Expedia and book the flight you've found. The price will be the same price you've found on this site.

Sneaky ways to beat the system

Here's a technique I've used many times, but now there's a computer app to make it easy.

Here's an example of how it works.

I used to fly to Las Vegas a lot (yeah, it was for work. I had an office in Las Vegas). A lot of times, I would be on a flight to Las Vegas that stopped in Phoenix. One time I was on my way to Phoenix and I noticed that the cost of my flight was going to be almost twice what I'd paid to go to Las Vegas with a stop in Phoenix three weeks earlier.

I booked a flight to Las Vegas, got off in Phoenix, and didn't get back on the flight going to Las Vegas.

There is one thing you have to be aware of when using this technique. That is you can only do this when you have only carry-on luggage. If you have checked a bag, your checked bag will go on to the destination you booked.

There are cheap flights to Las Vegas from a lot of cities. I ended up using this technique many times.

Now, instead of having to figure this out on your own, there's an app that will do it for you. Go to

https://SkipLagged.com/

Enter the city you want to go to, and they will do all the searching for you.

There's one other thing to be aware of when using this technique. It technically violates the airline's rules, and they could revoke your frequent flier privilege and your miles could be confiscated.

I've never heard of any airline doing this, but I no longer risk it with airlines that I have accumulated a large number of airline miles with. I've done it many times in the past with several different airlines.

Keep in mind that even though the technique may be against the airlines' rules, it is not illegal.

Speaking of going to Las Vegas, if you want to gamble on whether to buy your ticket now or wait and buy it later, there's an app that will give you the inside information and stack the deck in your favor.

Is the price of your flight going to get cheaper or more expensive if you wait to book? This app will tell you.

https://www.Hopper.com/

They claim to be 95% accurate even when booking up to a year in advance.

For example, I'll be going to Costa Rica in a few months, and the airfares I found are showing the prices to be less than half of what I paid last year. Wow. Should I go ahead and book my flights now before the prices go back up or are they going to get even cheaper if I wait? I used Hopper to find out.

Here's another sneaky way to get super cheap airline tickets

Airlines sometimes make mistakes when setting prices.

With the thousands of flights and fares changing weekly (and sometimes daily), airlines sometimes make a mistake and publish an incorrect price that's way too low. They usually discover the mistake and correct the price in a day or two, but they honor all of the tickets they sold at the ridiculously low price.

You would have to be lucky to find one of these mistakes, but you don't have to depend on luck. There's a website that will come to your rescue.

Check out https://www.SecretFlying.com/

I just checked, and I found a round-trip flight from Atlanta to Santiago, Chili for $62. Note, that's for a round-trip ticket.

How to book FREE airline tickets. There are two ways to get free airplane tickets, one is to use Frequent Flier miles. I try to fly mostly on one airline (Delta) but it's not always possible. Since I've flown over two million miles with Delta, I have a lot of unused Frequent Flier miles that I could use for free trips. I keep these for times when I want to make a last-minute trip since airlines usually charge a lot more for last-minute trips.

The other way to get free airline tickets is with credit card points. Be sure to have a credit card that gives you points that can be used for airline travel, and then charge as many expenses as you can to the card. Charge groceries, gas, and maybe your rent or mortgage payments.

Get an airline credit card with the airline you fly with the most often. They all offer thousands of bonus miles just for signing up. It's usually almost enough miles for a free flight.

When I say charge everything to your credit card so you can accumulate miles, I mean everything. I had a friend who charged her father's funeral to her credit card and then had enough miles to take a trip to Europe using her points.

Of course, pay your credit card balance every month or the interest will way more than offset any savings on your airline tickets.

If you're going to be doing some flying within a country you'll be visiting, wait until you get to that country and buy your ticket at that time.

You'll find that it's usually cheaper to buy a ticket to travel within a country while you're in the country than it is to buy it when you're outside of the country.

Be sure to check all the fees. Many of the airlines with cheap ticket prices charge a lot of money for luggage and other things. If you're paying $50 each for two bags, your cheap ticket might not be a good deal. Also, some airlines charge a fee for you to select your seat. Allegiant charges a $10 fee if you book your ticket online instead of at the airport.

To get the best prices, don't book a last-minute flight. By last minute I mean book your ticket at least two to three weeks before you plan to travel if possible. You'll pay more if you don't.

One final thing to do is switch to using a VPN (virtual private network) and select a third-world country as your location. Then check to see what the price of your ticket would be. Of course, it matters where you're flying to and from, but sometimes it also matters where the airlines think you live (and therefore how much money they think you have) as to what they can charge you for your ticket.

Dates: The best days to buy your ticket are Tuesday or Wednesday. Usually, the best days to fly are mid-week, Tuesday, Wednesday, or Thursday. Don't fly on Friday, Monday, weekends, or near or on holidays unless it's absolutely necessary.

Two last points

#1. Be sure to take the time to learn how to use the features of SkyScanner.com, Google.com/travel/explore, and any other apps or websites you're using. You'll learn how to save a lot of money if you can take advantage of all the features of these programs.

#2. Pack light. As in one small backpack and a fanny pack or purse. If you check two or three bags, your luggage fee could cost you more than your airline ticket. Whether you're going to be gone for three days or three months, a small backpack is all you need. If you find that you really need something when you get there, I'm sure you can find a place where you can buy the item.

Bottom line: If you want to fly cheap, do some research, have the right tools, and then use these websites and tools. And, of course, you have to be flexible.

Chapter 5

International Travel

"To travel is to live."

~ Hans Christian Andersen

The information and website links I referenced in the previous chapters all work for international travel too.

But here are some other techniques and tricks you can use for international travel.

I like international travel. You can learn so much about the world and the people in it.

"Travel is fatal to prejudice, bigotry, and narrow-mindedness, and many of our people need it sorely on these accounts. Broad, wholesome, charitable views of men and things cannot be acquired by vegetating in one little corner of the earth all one's lifetime."

~ Mark Twain

This quote describes international travel much better than I could describe it.

International travel is a great way to get new ideas. You'll find that a lot of things are done differently from what you're used to. Not necessarily better or worse—just different.

For example, in some parts of the world, everybody drives on the wrong side of the road. How insane is that?

Is international travel safe?

A lot of people are concerned about their safety when traveling outside of their native country. They feel safe in their own country but feel like they wouldn't be safe in another country.

I've heard people in Hong Kong say it's not safe when traveling in central China. When I was floating down rivers, crawling through caves, or just hiking in central

China, I heard people say they wouldn't feel safe in Hong Kong.

Likewise, I've heard people in Costa Rica say they wouldn't feel safe in Nicaragua and people from Nicaragua say they wouldn't feel safe in Costa Rica.

The truth is there are places in every city, even in the US, where I wouldn't want to be walking around at 2:00 a.m., but if you use a little common sense, international travel is just as safe as staying home.

I've slept in a tent in Africa, deep in the jungles of Uganda and heard distant drums at night and thought, *The natives are restless tonight,* but I didn't feel unsafe.

In a nutshell, everybody feels safe in an area they're familiar with and unsafe in areas they're not familiar with.

The key to low-cost international travel

To travel internationally, and do it inexpensively, you have to do a few things different from domestic travel.

First, your airfare will be a significant part of your travel expense, so make the most of your trip.

In addition to using all of the techniques in Chapter 4 that show you how to book cheap airfares, you also need to plan to make the most of the dollars you spent on your ticket.

One of the best ways to do this is to spend considerable time in the country or area you traveled to. Look at it this way. If you spent $600 for your round-trip airline ticket and only stayed for a long three-day weekend, you would be spending $200 a day for your airfare.

But if you stayed for a month, your airfare would only be adding $20 a day to your travel expenses.

If you rented an apartment for a month, you could get it for less than what it would cost you to stay in a hotel for a week, and maybe even less than what it would cost you for a three-day weekend at a nice hotel.

If you're traveling on Social Security, I assume you're retired, so you have time to stay somewhere for a month. **Get out of the habit of rushing.**

Be a temporary resident and not a tourist

If you go to a country and stay for three days, you're a tourist. You'll only see what tourists see. If you stay for a month, you're a temporary resident. It's a whole different experience.

G. K. Chesterton, a prolific British author of the 19th and 20th centuries (known as the Prince of Paradox), is famous for making two statements that may make you look at international travel in a different light.

Here are his two statements. Take a look at them and see what you think. Here is the first one.

"A true traveler lets the experience of a destination come to them, without manipulating it with expectations and prejudices."

Here is his second statement.

"The whole object of travel is not to set foot on foreign land: it is, at last, to set foot on one's own country as a foreign land."

In other words, you'll see and learn a lot more about your own country after you've experienced other countries to compare it to.

How to travel within a country

If you want to travel within a country, there are two options. In most countries, traveling by bus is inexpensive and interesting. You'll get to see the countryside and experience mingling with the natives. Even if you can't speak much of the language, you will find that you will be communicating with the locals through hand signs and using your smartphone to translate phrases.

If you want to travel longer distances and fly within a country, it's cheaper to buy your airline ticket to another town while you're in the country rather than buy the ticket while you're in the US.

I know a lot of people like to have everything planned and have all of their tickets purchased before they leave home, but you'll save money if you wait until you get to the country you want to visit to buy your tickets for travel within the country.

Also, who knows, after you get there, you may change your mind and decide to visit a different part of the country. Or you may catch a ride with a local or another visitor.

I've traveled a lot in different countries by catching a ride with a local or another traveler. You can also hire locals to take you places inexpensively. It's like getting a guided tour. Your driver will tell you things you would never learn if you were flying or taking a bus.

Be adventurous. Think outside the box. Talk to the locals and see what opportunities you come up with. You can sometimes meet up with other travelers and travel together and share expenses.

One other point. Before you leave on your trip, take the time to learn a little bit of the language of the country you're going to visit. Your trip will be much more interesting if you can speak and understand some of the language.

You won't understand everything that's said, but being able to pick up a few key words will come in handy.

I think every language program teaches you how to ask, "Where is the bathroom?" The problem is that almost none of them teach you how to understand the answer that you will receive when asking that question.

Once a year, travel to a foreign country

You're thinking about traveling or you wouldn't be reading this book. When you're making your travel plans, be sure to include traveling to a foreign country at least once a year.

International travel may get in your blood and you'll end up spending more time in foreign countries than you do in the US. It seems like each year I spend more time in foreign countries than I did the year before.

It's not a matter of cost; in fact, it's cheaper to live in a foreign country than it is to live in the US, so what are you waiting for? Start planning your international trip.

Before you leave, open a Charles Schwab account.

It's a money market deposit account. The main advantages for international travel are:

- You can use any ATM (at the end of the month they refund any fees that any ATM has charged you)
- There are no transaction fees
- There's no account minimum balance
- There are no monthly maintenance fees
- You get the Visa exchange rate, which is the best you can get

Two sites you should take a look at

https://www.numbeo.com/. This site is a great way to search for a destination based on the cost of living. It shows you the typical cost of everyday items, groceries, rent, etc.

https://NomadList.com/. If you're looking for a place to work and be a digital nomad, check out this website. It gives you various qualities of a city—including Internet speed, weather, crime rate, rent, and general cost of living.

Bottom line: You can buy a round-trip airline ticket, rent an apartment for a month, and pay for a month's worth of meals (by shopping in local markets and occasionally eating in a local mom and pop cafe). You can do all of this on one month's Social Security check if you use the techniques outlined in this book.

One other way that international living is inexpensive is that you are not trying to keep up with the Joneses (nobody is going to come visit you) and you don't need a guest room in the house or apartment you rent.

Chapter 6

Money Is Not Holding You Back. It's Fear

"I'm going to leave this one-horse town as soon as it's my turn to ride the horse."

~ A though had by a lot of people

When you start thinking about retiring and living a different kind of life, one of the first things you'll begin to think about is the money.

There are many places to travel, and some of them could get expensive, particularly if you're traveling in the conventional manner and being a tourist.

They could all get expensive if you let your travel expenses get out of hand. How much it costs to travel all depends on how you travel.

Every option we talked about could be very inexpensive or extremely expensive. So, yes, money could be a problem.

But looking on the bright side, you can travel to many places and live for a month or longer for less than it costs you to live your current lifestyle (and that includes your traveling expenses).

So, face the facts; money is not the issue. It's fear that's keeping you from traveling.

Maybe you could call it reservations or concerns. Those words mean about the same thing as fear, but they sound better. No one wants to say they're afraid of setting off on a travel adventure, but it's okay to have reservations.

Here are some of the fears (I mean reservations) you might experience when you think about traveling.

- Fear that you'll run out of money
- Fear that you'll blow what money you have and have to come home and admit that traveling was a big mistake

- Fear that you won't like traveling and then have to admit that you were wrong
- Fear of embarrassment when things don't work out
- Fear of not being safe
- Fear that your friends will think you're being totally irresponsible

"You probably wouldn't worry about what people think of you if you could know how seldom they do."

~ Olin Miller

In other words, stop worrying about what people think about you because, contrary to what you think, most people don't think about you at all.

Yes, it's fear

If you have a dream of traveling and you're not doing it yet, my guess is that fear is holding you back. It's not the money (maybe it's the fear of running out of money).

The idea of taking a risk conjures up feelings of fear. It's a normal and natural reaction. Fear helps keep us safe, but sometimes it's easy to let fear have more control over our actions than is warranted.

There's the fear of getting hurt, like the fear we had when we first started learning to ride a bicycle when we were kids. That's not the fear you're dealing with here. You don't think you might get hurt if you start traveling.

My guess is that your biggest fear is the unknown. It's like the fear of the dark when we were kids. We didn't know what was out there.

There's also the fear that it won't work out and then you'll have to listen to your family and friends saying, "I told you so." Even if they don't say it, you know they will be thinking it.

Most people don't want to admit it, but these are the fears that keep them from taking the plunge and living a different retirement lifestyle.

Keep reading, and I'll show you how you can be convinced that you really can make it work and how you can live your new retirement lifestyle on just your Social Security.

Something to think about

There's an old saying meant to remind you that you don't have to get involved with another person's drama.

The saying is, "*It's not my circus and not my monkeys.*" Sometimes it's good to keep that saying in mind.

But what if you look at your life and realize that this is your circus and those are your monkeys?

In other words, this is your life, and it's going to continue just as it is unless you make some changes.

Making a change involves taking a risk

A lot of people land a decent job and ride it until it's time to retire. Then they retire and continue to live in the same place and do the same thing they've done for years—which is basically nothing.

That's the safe way to live life, but you know what they say about the best-laid plans of mice and men. Things don't always work out the way you planned.

I just found out this week that a friend I had known for over 50 years was planning to retire at the end of this month. He got COVID-19 and died last week—two weeks before his planned retirement.

Almost everybody who died yesterday had plans for today.

If you think you want to travel one day—this is one day.

If you get your living expenses low, you'll have real security. Money fears will no longer exist.

You can start now and live a totally different life of traveling

Up until the last few years, retiring and traveling was not a realistic option for most people, but now technology (and a lot of other things) has changed all of that.

It's no longer a matter of whether you can afford to travel. The only question is, "Do you want to?"

Adventurous retirement living can be inexpensive because if you stop buying so much stuff that you don't need, you'll only have to pay for housing, food, travel expenses, insurance, maybe some medical expenses, a few personal items, and that's it. You don't need things and stuff. That's the bare minimum, but you'll probably want to spend a little more.

I'll get into all of that later in the book.

How I manage to travel the world

I have lived full-time in my motorhome for almost nine years now.

Living in an RV provides me the perfect opportunity (in my opinion) to travel the US and the world. There are places all over the US where I can stop and spend the night free of charge. I have heat, air-conditioning, hot water, a washer and dryer, a generator, solar, high-speed Internet, and most of the cable TV channels—all the conveniences I would have in a conventional house. I'm totally self-sufficient—and free to travel.

I can store my motorhome for $30 a month, cancel the collision insurance, and have no other expenses when I take off and travel internationally for three to six months.

If you want to know more about living the RV lifestyle, I've written a dozen books on the topic. Check them out at the back of this book or on my website, http://www.LifeRV.com/

How do I pay for my travels? I cover my expenses in three ways; I get my Social Security, I write books and sell them on Amazon, and I don't spend much. That way, I don't have to dip into my savings. I add to my savings each month while still traveling the world. You can do it too. In Chapter 12 I'll talk about ways to supplement your Social Security income.

Most people think they're locked into the way they're living now—even after they retire they don't make many changes.

All of our lives society and advertising have tried to brainwash us into believing that we need to keep working, accumulating more and more stuff, take a two-week vacation every year (when we can afford it), and be happy with that situation.

Most people have a job, a reasonably new car or two (with payments), and they think they've achieved the American Dream.

I think you've about decided that there must be more to life than this, and that's why you're reading this book to see if it's possible to stop working, retire, and travel on just your Social Security income.

As the title of the book implies, of course it is.

As you read this book, you will see that there's a whole new world waiting for you out there. You'll learn what it's like to live a life of travel in your retirement years. You'll also learn how you can afford to live this lifestyle while putting more money in savings every month than you're doing now.

One final thought: You can't plan everything regardless of how much time you take getting everything ready for your retirement and traveling adventure.

When I was in engineering school, almost all my time was spent learning how to design things. But when I started working as an engineer, I soon found out that I spent a lot more time testing designs than I ever spent doing the actual designs. I found out that that's the way engineering works. I don't remember ever testing anything in school.

You've planned everything. Your testing will start when you hit the road. You can't plan for everything. Well, you can. It's called an emergency fund. Don't leave home without it.

There may be valid reasons why you can't start traveling right now (aging parents you need to take care of, a business or house you need to sell, etc.), but don't let fear be one of the reasons you don't start traveling.

Fear is useful to help you make sure you've looked at all the factors involved, but it shouldn't be a reason not to take the plunge. Your retirement life can now be anything you want it to be. Traveling can be a big part of it. You can travel to anywhere you want, stay as long as you want to, and move when you want.

You'll have more freedom than you've ever had in your life. When you're traveling, most of the obligations, stress, other things that eat up your time and energy are left behind.

You will even have the freedom to stop living one retirement lifestyle and live a different lifestyle any time you want to. What a wonderful way to live—at least that's the way I see it.

Bottom line: Don't be afraid that something will go wrong. Accept the fact that for sure something will go wrong and then something else will go wrong. That's the traveling lifestyle. If you can't handle that, traveling is not for you. Fear will never go away completely, but as you gain confidence in your ability to handle the different situations that traveling throws at you, fear will lose its control over you.

Chapter 7

Don't Let Stuff Kill Your Travel Plans

"Don't wait. The time will never be just right."

~ Napoleon Hill

In this chapter, you'll find retirement advice that you won't get from any financial adviser. Here's that advice in a nutshell.

Get rid of your stuff and travel.

The biggest hindrance to enjoying travel for most people is their house and all the stuff they have accumulated.

The secret to traveling on just your Social Security income is to get rid of your stuff and then eliminate (or minimize) your expenses back home by selling your house or renting it out and eliminating most of your other expenses.

The other hindrance is that you may think you can't afford to travel. After reading this book, you will realize that you can afford to travel. You can probably do it for less than it costs you not to travel.

We are all pack rats by nature. We don't like to throw anything away. I think men tend to hold on to things because they think they might need them sometime.

A friend recently told me that he used something the other day he had kept in his garage since 1998. He kept it because he thought he might need it sometime. He was right. More than 20 years later, he needed it. Or at least he found a use for it.

It was a foot-long piece of mahogany wood. It was a beautiful piece of wood, and he couldn't bring himself to throw it away.

I think women hold on to things many times for sentimental reasons (men do to; they just don't admit it).

Of course, that's a broad generalization and men and women both hold on to things for many reasons—and sometimes for no reason at all.

I can't count the number of times I've had people tell me that they could never take off and travel because they have too much stuff.

They never say, "I choose to have too much stuff." They act like they were born that way and there is nothing they can do about it. They never look at the situation as a choice they made or the fact that the situation could ever be changed. It's just a fact of life—at least that's the way they see it.

Getting rid of stuff is the easy part

The hard part is deciding to get rid of stuff. It's easy after you decide you're going to do it and you want to do it.

In the next chapter, I will show you the easy way to get rid of all your excess junk (I mean valuable stuff) and be happy about it.

All the stuff you need to get rid of will fall into one of two categories: It's either something you might need one day or it's sentimental.

What about the stuff you might need?

There is always the possibility that a thing might be needed or come in handy some time. Almost everything could fit into that category.

When you get rid of most of your stuff, you will know what you have and where it is. It's a lot less stressful to say, "I don't have one of those," than to say, "I've got one somewhere, but I don't know where it is." It's a great feeling knowing everything you have and knowing where it is.

Nine years ago, I got rid of most of my stuff and moved into a 34-ft. Class A motorhome. I was sure that when I got rid of all the stuff I had accumulated I would need some of the things sooner or later, but I decided to accept that fact and not worry about it.

The truth is that, in nine years, I don't remember needing a single thing I got rid of. The day may come when I will say, "I wish I had kept that," but so far it's never happened.

What about sentimental things?

What to do with sentimental things is a big problem for a lot of people. Many people tell me that if they could deal with their mountain of sentimental items they could part with the other things.

The good news is there's an easy way to get rid of sentimental things that will leave you happy with the outcome.

Everyone who has used the techniques I will explain has been relieved and happy with the process and the outcome.

In the next chapter, I will explain in detail how to deal with all your sentimental things. You'll be amazed at how wonderfully well the technique works, but let's not get bogged down. You first have to decide that you want to part with your stuff. There's no point trying to figure out how to do it until you've decided that you want to do it.

The joy of having all of your junk gone

I talk to people all the time who have downsized from a 2,000-square-foot house to a 200-square-foot tiny house, boat, RV, or cabin, and believe it or not, they all say they don't miss a single thing they got rid of.

They say it's such a blessing to have all that stuff gone. They all had trouble letting go and getting rid of useful and sentimental things, but now that the items are gone, it's such a relief. With all their useless stuff gone, they are free.

Until you get rid of your stuff, you can't imagine the joy of having it all gone. Letting go of all the junk you've accumulated over the years gives you so much freedom.

Bottom line: Whether it's something that has sentimental value or something you think you might need someday, when it's gone, you will feel joy and freedom that's hard to imagine. Don't let stuff own you and control your life. Declare your independence from things and feel the joy. The next chapter will show you how to make it happen.

Chapter 8

How to Get Rid of Your Stuff

"A house is just a place to keep your stuff while you go out and get more stuff."

~ George Carlin

When people are getting ready to retire and start a new life and a new adventure, there's one problem everyone faces—what to do with all the somewhat valuable junk they have accumulated.

Even if you're not going to head off on a new life and start traveling immediately, now that you have some free time you need to get rid of a lot of clutter in your home and your life. This is the perfect time to do it.

All the time, I hear people say things such as, "I could never leave here. I have too much stuff."

They say it with the same conviction that they would say one leg was longer than the other. They act like they were born with all the stuff and there is nothing they can do about the situation.

When you get rid of all the useless junk (I mean valuable stuff) you have accumulated, you open up so many options for how you want to live your retirement. Even if you're still pondering your dreams and how you want to live your new retirement life, you know you want to do so traveling, even if you don't know where you want to go yet. If you are tied down by stuff, your traveling options are limited.

Get rid of your junk, and then, when you're free, you can decide what you want to do and where you want to go.

If you need even more help, I wrote a book called *Tidying Up.* In addition to showing you how to tidy up once and for all and never have to do it again, the book also shows you how to decide what to get rid of. The title of the book is

Tidying Up: The Magic and Secrets of Decluttering Your Home and Your Life

Since you're trying to get rid of stuff, you don't need another book around the house. As it says in the book, buy mostly eBooks from now on.

There is an eBook version of this book available. The eBook version is available from Amazon for $3.99 at the link below:

Amazon.com/dp/B01J6EVSR4

Read and follow the rest of this chapter and you probably won't need to buy the book, but if you need extra help the book can be your plan "B."

How to get rid of your stuff

Consider the following story to help you understand the concept.

A friend of mine told me that she wasn't ready to get rid of all her stuff when she decided to live a different lifestyle, so she stored everything in a barn on her parents' farm.

About a year later, the barn caught fire, and everything was destroyed. She said she should have been devastated, but she found herself feeling happy and didn't know why.

Then she realized the reason she was happy was that all her stuff was gone and she didn't have to feel guilty for getting rid of any of it. (The things she wanted she had taken with her.)

It wasn't that she wanted any of the stuff; she just didn't want to get rid of it at the time. I think that describes a lot of us.

If you say, "I choose to have all of this stuff," then you own the situation or problem. It's easier to deal with the situation when you look at it that way.

Here are the steps to getting rid of your stuff

Your stuff can all be classified into one of four categories—A, B, C, and D.

Category A: Things you are going to use and take with you. If you're going to be traveling full-time, that will be almost nothing more than what will fit into a backpack.

Category B: These are the things you can sell—your dining room table and chairs, the sofa you bought two years ago, and your riding lawnmower. You can sell almost everything and it doesn't take long to do it. Selling all this stuff is an excellent way to bring in some extra cash.

Craigslist is a great way to sell larger items. If you price the items right and include pictures, they will usually sell within a week. If an item doesn't sell within a week, lower the price by at least a third and list it again.

Be sure to list a phone number where you can be reached most of the time. When someone is ready to buy something, they will call another person selling essentially the same type of item you're offering if they can't get you on the phone.

I have sold a lot of items using Craigslist. The system works great. You get a fair price and you get it sold quickly.

For smaller items that you can ship, you can use eBay or Facebook MarketPlace. For Craigslist, Facebook MarketPlace, and eBay, be sure to show several good quality pictures. Pictures help items sell quickly.

With eBay, you can set a reserve price or auction it off and take what you get. After all, usually, whatever it sells for is what it's worth, and that's what you wanted to do in the first place—sell the item for whatever it's worth.

Category C: These are the things that you put in a garage sale on a Saturday and then take what doesn't sell to Goodwill. This way, at the end of the day, everything in this category is gone.

Category D: This category is for sentimental things. A few of these things you may want to put in a storage unit, but very few. Pictures and photo albums can all be scanned and placed on a thumb drive or stored in the cloud. If you don't know how to do this, some businesses offer this service at a reasonable price.

Most people think things on this list are the hardest to get rid of, but these items can be the easiest to get rid of if you follow the procedure described below.

First, decide who you want to have each of these things when you're dead and gone. (I know you consider that to be a long way off but think about it this way anyway.) Then give the items to them now. If they won't take the things now, you know what will happen to them as soon as you're gone. They'll give them to Goodwill, sell them in a garage sale or throw them away.

If you have a few items that you want your grandchildren to have when they're grown, you can put these items in storage if you can't convince their parents to keep the things for them.

I know it's hard to accept that many things you cherish will not even be considered worth keeping by other people when you're gone. That's just a fact. Don't blame your relatives. It's not their responsibility or duty to like or value the same things you like.

Many of the things you will be giving people will be things they will love and enjoy having. By giving them the items now, you'll get to see them enjoy the things and you'll know the items went to the people you wanted to have them.

Don't just put things in storage—at least not more than what will fit in the smallest storage unit they make.

If you do put things in a storage unit, consider getting rid of even those things a year from now. Some people have found it easier to get rid of sentimental items in a two-step process like this, but don't let it drag out for years and still have your belongings in storage.

In other words, put those things you think you can't part with in storage for one year. At the end of a year, decide if you want to continue your traveling lifestyle. If so, give everything in storage that you're not going to use to your relatives. If they don't want the items, sell them. If something doesn't sell, give it to Goodwill or throw it away.

It will feel like a tremendous burden is lifted from your shoulders when you have gotten rid of all the stuff you don't need.

There is some wiggle room

Now that I've convinced you to get rid of most of your stuff and shown you how to do it, let me back up and tell you that you do have a little bit of wiggle room.

Many retirees get a small storage unit and they keep a few things there that they're not ready to get rid of yet.

I know one couple who took a picture of their empty storage unit and then threw a party and invited their friends to help them celebrate the big occasion. It was a fun time.

Plan your party now to celebrate your freedom from **stuff**.

One final point: Don't go through your stuff and decide what to throw away. Go through it and decide what to keep.

The best way to determine what to keep is to ask yourself, "Does this bring me joy?" If you're truthful with yourself, you'll decide that most items don't really bring you any joy, so don't keep them. It's that simple.

One person told me that they followed this procedure of getting rid of everything that didn't bring them joy. They said they got rid of their treadmill, their electricity bill, the lawnmower, the alarm clock, and a long list of things. Keep in mind that you may not like an item but you may like what it does for you.

Bottom line: You have all this stuff because you choose to have it. Therefore, you can choose to get rid of it. You may not believe it now, but it's such a relief when you get rid of all the stuff you've been hanging on to for years.

Chapter 9

Simplify and Go

"Our life is frittered away by details . . . simplify, simplify."

~ Henry David Thoreau

People have wanted to travel since the beginning of time. They want to know what's over the next hill or around the next bend in the road.

Now that you have your Social Security income (or will soon have it) you'll have many freedoms and opportunities. You'll have to decide which ones to say no to and which crazy dreams are worth pursuing.

The best way to start traveling is just to simplify and go. Work things out while you're on the road.

A lot of people dream about traveling someday but they never get around to doing it. It's not that they make a decision not to travel. It's just that they don't make a decision.

You'll never have all the information

Every decision you make for the rest of your life will be made with incomplete information. Accept that fact and your life will be a lot less stressful.

Do a reasonable amount of research, make your decision, and hit the road. You can make changes as you learn more and gain more experience.

One of the things I like best about traveling is the experiences I have and the unknowns. If I knew everything that was going to happen and everything I was going to do and experience, it would soon turn into a boring trip. There would be no adventure.

You'll have to decide if you want to travel full-time or if you want to take a trip now and then. And whether you want to travel around the US or do some international travel, it doesn't matter. It doesn't have to be one or the other. You can do some of both. The only important thing is that you make a decision and hit the road.

When you make a decision, it doesn't have to be permanent, and it probably won't be.

Whatever you do, don't just take off for a weekend and call that traveling. Your first trip should be for at least two weeks. A month would be better.

You're not going on a vacation. There's a big difference between going on a vacation and living a different traveling lifestyle.

A quality-of-life decision

Deciding to start traveling and living a different lifestyle is a decision that's easy to put off. Some people think about traveling from time to time but they never actually decide to do it or not to do it. They just don't decide.

I like to think of it as making a "quality-of-life decision." Will you have a happier life living like you are now or would you be happier traveling?

When you first started thinking about deciding to travel, it probably wasn't to see the world or escape the monotonous life you lived. Those may have been contributing factors for sure. But my guess is you wanted to start living a life of adventure.

Here are three questions to ask yourself about whether to travel or not.

1. **Does this align with other big goals in my life?**

   When we think about big goals, we tend to think about decisions we were faced with in our younger life when we first got out of school or got married. We were faced with big decisions about our life then, but since then maybe there haven't been a lot of big decisions—we just kind of went with the flow.

   We all still have dreams. Some big—like traveling the world. Some small—like should I get a dog (not if you're going to be traveling)?

   A quality-of-life decision aligns with those big and small dreams and pushes you closer to them or further away from them.

2. **When I make this decision, will it feel light or heavy?**

   This is just a fancy way of asking, "Will making this decision make me feel happy?"

   We've all had the experience of making a decision and afterward suddenly feeling the weight of the world lifted off our shoulders. Maybe it was a weight you didn't even realize you were carrying, but you sure knew when it was lifted.

The burden of making big decisions is heavy. That's why thinking about how you will **feel** after you make the decision is so important and it will help you make the decision.

3. **Am I ready to start on this journey?**

   For most of us, this is the scariest question of all because the answer is always, "I don't know."

   There are so many unknowns, but that's part of the adventure and what makes the journey exciting.

You always have the option of doing nothing and continuing to live your life the way you're living now, but obviously the life you're living now is not making you completely happy and there's no excitement in your life—or at least not enough.

You want something different or you wouldn't be reading this book.

Bottom line: When it comes to deciding whether to travel, where to travel, and how to travel, listen to your soul, inner voice, gut feel, heart, or whatever you want to call it, but after doing your research you'll know if traveling is in your blood or not. Since you're reading this book, I'm pretty sure it is.

Chapter 10

Loneliness and Emotional Aspects of Traveling

"It's tough to make predictions, especially about the future."

~ Yogi Berra

You will meet many interesting people when you're traveling, but there will be times when you will feel lonely. When you're in your room by yourself at night or eating lunch alone at a little cafe you might feel lonely.

You will learn to deal with and appreciate your own company. Learn to love yourself.

The **thought** of solo travel will likely make you feel lonelier than actually traveling solo.

When you're traveling solo, you will be pushed out of your comfort zone in a heartbeat. That's a good thing. That's the whole purpose of traveling, to experience new things. You can't do that if you stay in your comfort zone.

You don't want to go to a different city or some foreign country and stay in a Holiday Inn. You might as well stay in your town or even in your own home. It will be too familiar. You won't experience anything new. So, accept feeling a little lonely as an encouragement to do and experience something different. After all, that's the whole purpose of traveling.

Say hello to strangers. A lot of travelers are traveling solo, and they are just as lonely as you are. When you're staying in a hostel, almost everybody there is a solo traveler.

There is a difference between loneliness and being alone. Being lonely is not healthy, but spending some time alone is.

Humans need some alone time and most people don't get enough of it.

Distance makes you appreciate all of the important people in your life.

When you're traveling alone, you're always going to make lots of new acquaintances, and some of them will even become friends.

There's something liberating about traveling to a place where nobody knows who you are.

Alone time is not a bad thing. Some of my most creative ideas have come when I'm alone. In fact, I think all of them have. I'm not creative when I'm not alone.

Travelers are incredibly open. They are likely lonelier than you are. Many times, locals are the same way. They want to talk to somebody.

If you're feeling lonely, change your surroundings. If you're still feeling lonely, change your surroundings again.

One thing you can do when you're in a strange town and you feel lonely is to sign up for a language class or a cooking class, or any other class that interests you.

Doing this will get your mind occupied, allow you to meet people, and give you a sense of accomplishment.

Hostels almost became extinct at the height of the COVID epidemic, but they have come back and are popular again. You're never lonely in a hostel. You can talk with the people in your dorm room or hang out in the common area and meet people. Almost everybody there is traveling solo and they are all super friendly and open to meeting people.

I love staying in hostels. They are dirt cheap (unless there are two you—then they're dirt cheap times two, which could be getting close to the cost of a low-cost hotel room).

Bottom line: Consider your alone time as something to look forward to. Maybe try being even more isolated. Spend a day with a good book and no Internet, TV, newspaper, or cell phone. Just enjoy being with yourself. Yes, there are times when you will want (and need) to be with other people, but take advantage of the times you have to be alone and enjoy and cherish them.

Chapter 11

Solo Traveling

"The man who goes alone can start today, but he who travels with another must wait till that other is ready."

~ Henry David Thoreau

I talk to people all the time who tell me that they would love to travel if they had someone to travel with.

Obviously, the don't realize the joys of solo travel.

I've been traveling solo full-time for nine years. I love solo travel. There are so many advantages to this way of traveling.

Just because your spouse (or significant other) is no longer around (for whatever reason), it's no reason for you to stop living your life.

You may not want to do the same thing the two of you had planned. It just wouldn't be the same. But there are so many other places to visit and experience.

There are a lot of advantages to solo travel

- It's easier to plan things when you only have to please yourself.
- It's less expensive for one person to travel and live.
- When you travel solo, you can enjoy freedom as you've never experienced it before.
- You get to do what you want to do.

Things you should do if you're traveling internationally as a solo traveler

- Get a SIM card so your phone will work in the country you'll be visiting.
- Download a map of the country and the city you'll be visiting so you'll have a map when you don't have a Wi-Fi signal.
- When you arrive at a new location, send a message to a friend or relative and let them know where you are.

Realize that staying in the same place and doing the same thing (essentially living in the past) is the worst possible option.

Your life should not be about checking things off of a bucket list. You don't have to visit every state.

Spend a month, two months, or even a year in one country and you will have fun and experience so much.

When you're considering whether to travel solo or not go, make a list of 20 places you would like to visit someday.

Then realize that if you don't go to these places by yourself, you will probably never go. Also, remember that it's better to be alone than in bad company.

Traveling solo is a wonderful way to travel. Imagine the freedom to do what you want to do when you want to do it.

Important words of wisdom for solo travelers

Below are the things that solo travelers should ever be mindful of whether they're traveling in the US or foreign countries. These points are not in any particular order.

- Always walk around looking and feeling confident. Don't ever look confused. If you do, scammers will recognize this look and pounce on you.

- Consider taking a local tour. I don't like organized trips where everything is planned, but I sometimes like to take a one-day or half-day tour of a city I'm visiting. It's an excellent way to learn a lot about the city. Also, I've noticed that a lot of the people on these tours are solo travelers. It's a good way to meet fellow solo travelers.
- Staying in a hostel is a great way to meet other solo travelers. During the COVID-19 pandemic, the hostel industry almost died, but now, with the vaccine, hostels are getting popular again. You'll find mostly young people staying in hostels, but I like being around young people. They are lively, full of ambition, and energetic (even though they are sometimes loud and don't go to bed as early as I like to).
- Eating at food courts, sidewalk cafes and street carts where there are common tables nearby for people to sit at and eat is a safe way to meet locals and fellow solo travelers.
- Trust your gut. If a person or situation doesn't seem safe or something doesn't seem right, get out of the situation immediately.

- As soon as you get on a plane, bus, or in your car to start your trip, half of your fears and worries will disappear.
- Pack light. One small backpack and maybe a fanny pack is all you need.
- If you're not prepared to lose it, don't take it. This will allow you to be more carefree and will eliminate a lot of stress and worries. I don't carry my best computer with me when I travel, and I keep all my files backed up in the cloud using a service called Carbonite. I can download all my files to another computer anywhere in the world.
- Keep your phone battery charged and carry a small device that you can plug into your phone and recharge the battery. You don't ever want to be traveling and not be able to get in touch with other people. The one I carry in a fanny pack is about half the size of my phone and will allow me to recharge my phone three times.
- Carry a copy of your driver's license and your passport with you, and keep a copy in a safe place in your room.
- Have more than one credit card, and don't keep them all in the same place. Also, don't keep all of your cash in one place.

- Don't drink too much. Even better, drink very little when you're out by yourself.
- Don't take expensive jewelry with you. Don't even take fake jewelry that looks expensive.

One more thing

If you don't want to continue living your life by yourself, you have to take some steps to make something happen.

Realize that you are a lot more likely to meet someone who will have your same interests and want to live and enjoy the same life you're living when you're traveling.

After all, if you could find someone to share your dreams with by living the way you're living now don't you think you would have already found them?

What about security?

Safety and security concerns mainly grow out of fear of the unknown. It's human nature to fear the unknown.

If there were no unknowns, there would be no adventure. How much fun would that be?

Here's what Helen Keller had to say about security:

"Security is mostly a superstition. It does not exist in nature, nor do the children of men as a whole experience it. Avoiding danger is no safer in the long run than outright exposure. Life is either a daring adventure or nothing."

~ Helen Keller

If Helen Keller wasn't afraid, why should we ever be shaking in our boots?

When you realize that security is not a problem for you as a solo traveller, what else is there to worry about?

You could say, "What about money?" I'll cover that in the next chapter, and you will see that money is not something to worry about at all.

You don't have to travel alone

Take another look at old Henry's quote at the beginning of this chapter about the fact that when you're alone, you can start when you want to. Ponder what he said.

I like traveling alone, but if you don't feel comfortable traveling alone, the world is full of single people who feel the same way you do and don't want to travel alone.

If you don't know anyone personally that you are compatible with and would like to travel with or someone interested in traveling at the same time and to the same place you want to travel to, below are two websites that will help you find a suitable traveling companion. These are not dating sites.

You can use the service at www.SeniorMatch.com. All members are over 50, and the majority are retired professionals, or they soon will be retired.

Another alternative is www.TravelBuddy.com, which has 1.6 million members worldwide. Unlike SeniorMatch, there is no age limit on TravelBuddy—and it's free.

You may decide that you like traveling alone. It does have its advantages.

Bottom line: Don't live in the past with thoughts of **what if** or **if only**. Grab life by the horns and live your life to the fullest. You are entirely free to do it.

Traveling solo is one of the most remarkable ways to enjoy and experience life.

So, as Mark Twain said, *"Throw off the bowlines. Sail away from the safe harbour. Catch the trade winds in your sails. Explore. Dream. Discover."*

Chapter 12

Ways to Stretch Your Social Security Income

"Let us all be happy and live within our means, even if we have to borrow to do it."

~ Artemus Ward

There are two basic ways to stretch your Social Security income—spend less or make a little extra money. You can easily do both, and in this chapter I'll show you how.

How to spend less money

If you like to go shopping, buy new clothes, buy the latest gadgets, go to concerts and sporting events, like new cars, want the newest cell phone, and like to eat out all the time, you're going to end up spending as much (and maybe even more) money after you retire as you're spending now because. . .

Retiring won't change who you are

You have to make a conscious effort to change your ways. One of the first things you have to do to retire and travel on your Social Security is to find ways to live and not spend so much money.

Stop buying stuff

One of the best ways to get your living expenses down is to stop buying stuff. Going shopping should no longer be a form of entertainment.

Adopt the habit of getting rid of something every time you buy something new. If you buy a new pair of shoes, throw out an old pair. When you're considering buying something, ask yourself, "What am I going to throw away?" That may keep you from purchasing the item being considered.

I don't mean you should just cut back. I'm saying that you should stop buying stuff altogether (well, almost).

How retirees save money

Your best option to save money is to make changes in areas where most of your money is being spent. You can't save any money by cutting back on how much you spend on shoe polish because if you totally eliminated shoe polish it wouldn't save enough to matter.

I know I'm being facetious, but I'm doing it to make a point. It reminds me of the mother who said to her kid, "If I've told you once, I've told you a million times. Don't exaggerate."

I got off track. Let's get back to how retirees save money.

To save money, you have to cut back in the areas where you are spending a lot of money. Keep detailed records of every penny you spend for a month or so and you might be surprised at the areas where you're spending money.

Armed with this information, you can make informed decisions about where and how to cut back on your spending.

When you're retired, here are three areas you need to look at closely

1. **Eating out:** First, don't eat out very often. Make it a special occasion. If you eat out a lot, then it's no longer a special occasion. Also, skip the chain restaurants and tourist places. Eat at the local mom and pop places and you will get to experience the area's real cuisine.

2. **Don't waste food:** Even if you eat most of your meals at home, you may still be wasting a lot of money by throwing away too much food. One way to save a lot on food is to start planning every meal by looking in the refrigerator and seeing what leftovers you have and then thinking about what you would need to add to those leftovers to make a good meal. We're all guilty of leaving leftovers in the back of the refrigerator too long and then throwing them out. And we all know ways to save when buying food. We just don't do it. Cut out junk food, shop at discount stores like Aldi, buy mostly real food—beans, rice, veggies—and cut back on protein and high-priced cuts of meat. Also, watch fruits and veggies closely and be sure to eat them before they go bad.

3. **Save money on clothes:** You probably have enough clothes to last you a long time before you will ever

need to buy more. When you're traveling, you're more interested in clothes that are comfortable and functional—you don't worry about what's in style.

And when you do need more clothes, go to Goodwill or a thrift shop. There was a time when people tried to keep it a secret that they shopped at Goodwill. Now they brag about it. I was sitting around a campfire not long ago in an RV park and one woman commented to another that she liked her shirt. Her reply was, "I got it at Goodwill for four dollars."

A friend of mine's father died recently. My friend had gotten rid of all of his suits and sports coats when he retired. He went to Goodwill and paid $5 for a sports coat to wear to his father's funeral, and then, on the way home from the funeral, he stopped and donated it back to Goodwill.

If you can get these three categories (eating out, wasting food, and clothes) down to zero, your retirement lifestyle won't be expensive at all.

Of course, you can't get them down to zero, but, for most people, these expenses can be cut way down and without any decrease in quality of life or enjoyment—just follow the advice I've outlined.

One other point—don't be a tourist. This topic is covered in great detail in the next chapter, but I wanted to mention it briefly here because it's important to the topic of this chapter.

One of the best ways retirees have found to save money is to stop being a tourist. Many new retirees spend a lot of money when they first retire because they act like they're on vacation and do things as though they are a tourist—eating out a lot, spending money on tourist attractions, and just generally acting like they're on vacation.

Remember that you're not on a full-time vacation and you're not a tourist. If you do all of the tourist things, you're going to blow your budget in a hurry. I've had several retirees tell me that they spent a lot more money the first year they were retired than they do now. They say it's more fun to be a temporary resident in an area than it is to be a tourist, and, of course, a lot less expensive.

Save and splurge

One advantage of saving a lot of money is that it gives you more money to spend on things that make you happy. You can do a few tourist things and buy a few gadgets, but only a few.

I don't spend much on clothes and I don't eat out a lot. One way I do save money when I eat out is that since I don't eat nearly as much as I used to, rather than leaving the uneaten food on my plate and wasting it, I get a to-go box and take it home.

When I eat out, I can usually get two meals out of what I order, which cuts the price way down.

Another area where I have to watch my budget is that I like gadgets, especially electronic things.

How to make extra money when you're retired

Employers now recognize retirees as being hard-working, dependable employees. They're eager to hire them to work part-time.

Lots of other income-producing opportunities for retirees will be described later in the book.

If you earn money while you're collecting Social Security, your income might be reduced if you start receiving Social Security before you reach full retirement age (FRA), the age when you qualify to collect 100 percent of the maximum benefit allowed based on your earnings history. The FRA is 66 to 67, depending on when you were born.

Until then, Social Security doesn't consider you fully "retired." If you make more than a certain amount from work, a portion of your benefits will be deducted from you payment.

Once you reach FRA, there is no cap on how much you can earn and still receive your full Social Security benefit.

The earnings limits are adjusted annually for national wage trends. In 2020, you lose $1 in benefits for every $2 earned over $18,240. Keep in mind that you do have to pay Social Security on the earnings.

The earnings cap applies only to income from work. It does not count investments, pensions, annuities.

In other words, you can make almost $20,000 extra and still draw your full Social Security income.

Would an extra $20,000 a year make your retirement more enjoyable?

How to make an extra $20,000 a year

The term "Digital Nomad" is popular these days. It more or less means a person who travels and makes money using their computer. You can be a digital nomad. The rest of this chapter will tell you how.

The two best sources of information for how to make money while traveling is the book, *Road Cash*, by Bill

Myers (available on Amazon) and Camille Attell's websites at https://www.MoreThanAWwheelin.com/.

I'll break the work and techniques for making money down into two basic categories. I do some of both.

#1. Swap your time for dollars.

This technique's advantages are that you usually get paid quickly, you're sure to be paid (you do the work and you get paid—there's no risk), and you typically have a lot of freedom. You can do the work whenever and wherever you want to (as long as you meet the completion deadline if there is one).

The disadvantage is that you're not making a lot of money for the hours you put in ($10 to $20 an hour). But since you don't have to spend time getting ready for work or traveling to and from work, maybe the pay is not so bad after all.

Another disadvantage is that when you're not working, you're not getting paid. You might think, *Duh, isn't that true for all jobs?*

Not necessarily. Later I'll talk about work where you do the work one time and get paid month after month for years and may end up making hundreds or thousands of dollars an hour (such as writing books, developing online courses, or producing videos).

Here are some of the types of work you can do that fit into the first category of swapping your time for dollars.

Teach English. You can make about $16 to $20 an hour doing this. The requirements are that you have a bachelor's degree (in anything), have English as your primary language, and that you're available to start work early (by 6:30 a.m. Eastern time for most of the jobs) because you will mainly be teaching kids in China in their evening time.

Here are two companies to work for if you want to teach English online.

- VIPkid.com

  Forbes ranked this company as one of the top companies to work for.

- DaDa.com

  I've heard good things about this company too, but I've never worked for either one of them.

Do remote work. An excellent example of this type of work is where you have a job that allows you to work from home (and home can usually be anywhere, even in a foreign country, but you'll probably need a reliable Internet connection most of the time).

One of the most significant disadvantages of this type of work is that you may not have much time freedom. You may need to be available at certain hours of the day. This may fit your needs and it may not.

Do freelance work. The main advantages of doing freelance work are that you can work from anywhere, you can work your own hours (there are usually deadlines to meet), you get paid as soon as the job is finished, and you can usually get plenty of work (as long as you set your rate low enough).

The disadvantages are that you are constantly looking for work. You usually have to meet deadlines and the income you make is modest.

Here are four places to get customers who are looking for freelance workers.

https://www.fiverr.com/—I have used this website for years to get work done. I've had book covers designed, proofreading done, editing done, formatting, found graphic designers, and the list goes on and on.

You can check out the Fiverr.com website to see the list of services being offered. Which ones of these could you do?

I have not used the other services listed below, but check them out.

https://www.freelancer.com/

https://www.peopleperhour.com/v4

http://upwork.com/

If you want to learn a skill (or get better at a skill), here's what I recommend.

Three Ways to Learn a Skill

- YouTube videos
- https://www.udemy.com/

  Be sure to check the number of reviews and the star rating when selecting a course to make sure you're getting a good course.
- https://www.linkedin.com/ (formerly Lynda.com)

Watching YouTube videos is my first choice. I do this all the time. Also, check out the courses on Udemy.com. They have several online courses for just about any topic. The prices are as low as $15.

You can teach music, do handyman chores, paint houses, do yard and landscaping work, do car detailing, or do bookkeeping work. You can also do writing projects and write articles, newsletters, emails, or sales letters. The amount you will get paid per hour for this work will probably be low, but remember you're not doing this work for a living. You're doing it for a little extra money.

The jobs may not be jobs you would want for a career, but when you're not depending on them to put food on your table, you might find them enjoyable. Many people tell me that they find the jobs interesting and enjoy getting out and meeting new people. For the manual jobs, many people say they like the exercise.

#2. Do the work once and get paid forever (more or less).

Here are some ways to make this happen.

Write books. I can hear you now saying that you're not a writer. I'm an engineer. I'm not a writer either. I never made a grade higher than a "C" in a college English class in my life. I'm sure some of the readers of my books have said, "I can tell that."

Some of my best-selling books are books that I wrote four or five years ago. They still bring in money every month.

When I write books like this one, I write just like I'm talking to a friend. Then I hire a proofreader to get rid of my many errors. I also hire somebody to design a cover. Proofreaders don't get paid much, book cover designers don't either, but writers do.

If you like to write fiction, you can make more money than us non-fiction writers. The fiction writers I know make about ten times more for each book than I do, but I don't have the skill or interest in writing fiction.

If you write novels, it's a good marketing idea to write a series like Mark Twain did with his Huckleberry Finn series. He had the same characters only different adventures.

If you write a series, write them so that each one stands alone and they don't have to be read in any order. That way, anytime someone buys one book, there's a good chance they will purchase other books in the series.

Create courses to sell. These usually consist of four to eight videos and a dozen or more written lessons. If you don't have a list to sell to, you can get other people who have a list in your niche to sell the course and usually pay them about a 50% commission. Courses usually sell for $95 to $395. You can also sell your courses on the Udemy.com website. They charge a 50% commission.

Bottom line: Follow the advice in this chapter and you can cut your expenses way down and have more money for traveling. And when you're not spending much money and you're making extra money, you'll find that the traveling life is so much more enjoyable.

Chapter 13

Don't Be a Tourist—Maybe a Little Bit

"I hate small towns because once you've seen the cannon in the park, there's nothing to do."

~ Lenny Bruce

There are some tourist things that you'll want to do. If you get close to the Grand Canyon, Niagara Falls, or the Eiffel Tower, by all means see them, but don't spend a lot of money on a special tour.

If you see these things, you will be a tourist for sure, but that's alright. It's okay to be a little bit of a tourist, but that's enough. After seeing the few tourist things that you should see, stop being a tourist.

There are a lot of non-tourist things you will enjoy a lot more. What about the little bakery around the corner from where you were staying that had those amazingly delicious warm bagels every morning?

What about the time you spent talking to the food cart owner where you got your lunch almost every day?

Do you remember what he said his plans were for next year? What is his daughter going to do when she graduates from college in the spring?

"The traveler sees what he sees. The tourist sees what he has come to see."

~ Gilbert K. Chesterton

This quote is so true. It means the tourist visits a place to see the attraction he came to see. It implies a traveler visits to experience the culture, see the country, the city, and the people—the way they are.

A few attractions are worth seeing, but most of them are not, and for sure, they are not the only thing in the area worth seeing and experiencing.

If you just wanted to see the tourist attractions, you could watch the travel channel.

If you see a tourist attraction, you can check it off of your bucket list. I don't have a bucket list. There is absolutely nothing I have a deep desire to see or do, but I love to travel and experience whatever the world has to offer.

When I travel, I want to experience the area, the people, their lives, and, most of all, the culture. Whether I'm in Louisiana bayou country, a West Texas oil field, or the French Riviera, I want to experience the area and the people.

I was in a foreign country once and a woman was cutting my hair. Her husband came in and we got to talking. They ended up inviting me to come to their house for Sunday lunch. I've never had a barber in the US invite me to come to his house for Sunday lunch.

I like sidewalk cafes, coffee shops, food carts, hiking trails, farmers' markets, and mom and pop cafes.

When I'm in an area, I want to be a temporary resident—not a visitor and, for sure, not a tourist. In many places you visit, it will be evident that you're not a local, but you can still be a resident, even if you are a temporary resident.

When you adopt this traveling mindset, you'll be surprised how much more enjoyable your traveling will become. It will be a whole different world.

Three things to do everywhere you travel

Whether I'm traveling to a foreign country or just a city I haven't been to before, below are the three things I always like to do.

1. See something special. What's unique about the area?
2. Do something that's fun and interesting. Hike on an interesting trail, float down a river, stand under a waterfall, or whatever you can do there that you're not likely to be able to do in other areas.
3. Eat something or eat at a place that's unique to the area.

These are the three thing you'll remember about any area. You don't have to do these things just one time. You can eat at several places, and experience seeing or doing more than one thing.

I'm not talking about seeing and doing the things that tourists see and do. Do the non-tourists (and usually free) things in the area.

Keep a journal

Every day take a few minutes to jot down any information that you think you might one day like to remember.

For example, what was the name of that little restaurant you liked so much? What was the name of the owner (or waitress) who was so friendly and helpful?

Happiness is a place that doesn't care how you get there, but traveling is one way to get there for sure.

Bottom line: Whether you're traveling in the US or internationally, change your thinking. Don't be a tourist. Try as hard as you can to be a temporary resident. You'll have a whole different experience.

Chapter 14

The Internet Now Makes Travel Affordable and Enjoyable

"Adventure is worthwhile in itself."

~ Amelia Earhart

To get the most out of your travel experience, use the Internet. It's that simple.

In almost every chapter of this book, I provide links to websites that will make your travel experience more enjoyable and help you travel with less hassle.

To get the most out of your travels, make a list of websites you use frequently and store them on your computer and cell phone. Then, by all means, use them. Your life will be so much simpler and your travels will be more enjoyable.

www.YouTube.com—This is one of the most underused websites for travelers. People use it for everything else but not so much when it comes to helping them with their travel.

There are videos where people tell you why you should or shouldn't visit a particular city or state or country. There are videos showing tours of different cities, states, and countries.

Printed maps are almost a thing of the past. You can find maps of cities or areas anywhere in the world on the Internet.

The two most popular websites I use that have good maps are:

https://www.google.com/maps

https://www.mapquest.com/

I like to download maps of places I'm going to my phone so if I'm in a place and don't have a Wi-Fi signal I can still see the map.

Don't buy a travel package

The world is full of companies wanting to sell retirees travel packages. A travel package is a good way to see the most in the shortest amount of time (but **not** for the least amount of money).

You also don't have to think when you're traveling on a pre-arranged package tour. When I'm traveling, I want to make my own decisions. I want to decide how long I'll stay in a place and when I'm ready to go on to the next place. I may fall in love with a place and want to stay for a week. It's happened.

At this point in your life, you have time, so you don't need (or want) to cram everything into seven days.

Get on the Internet, do your research, plan your travel, and so what if you miss seeing something that you later find out that everybody says you have to see. You don't want to be a tourist anyway.

If you're planning an international trip, make sure you don't travel to a location that the US government doesn't recommend you travel to. Find out where not to go at this website.

https://www.state.gov/travel/com

You can also use this site to find out about passports, visa requirements, etc.

Since you're a vagabond traveler, you don't want to check into a hotel, sit on the beach out front or in the lobby, and then catch a tour bus the next morning.

You had rather spend time in a local coffee shop talking to the locals and the other vagabond travelers. Find out what they're doing, what they've done, and what they plan to do.

In almost every country and many cities in the US you'll run across people (usually single) called "digital nomads." They travel around the world (generally staying in one place for weeks or months at a time). They make their living by doing gig work on their computers, such as website design, proofreading, graphic design, book cover design, logo designs, etc. They do any location-independent work they can do on their computers. Talk to them and you'll find them interesting.

They know all the great places to get a good, low-cost meal and they know where the safe, clean, and low-cost places to stay are. They'll for sure know where to get the best Wi-Fi signal. They'll have a world of information about the area. They'll also turn you on to websites in the area that will be useful.

Bottom line: All the information in the world (and about the world) is now available on the Internet and available to you on your computer and cell phone. I like to have a little computer with me when I'm out walking around or hanging out. I have a little one that fits in my fanny pack. It keeps me connected to the world. Of course, you can do the same thing with your cell phone; you'll just have a smaller screen.

Chapter 15

You Have to be Healthy and Stay in Shape to Travel

"Be careful when reading health books; you may die of a misprint."

~ Mark Twain

First of all, let me state that I'm not a doctor, and I don't play one on TV, so nothing in this chapter should be considered medical advice. What I'm saying in this chapter is just my opinion.

Many people retire and soon wind up depressed with no interest or purpose in life. They soon experience a rapid decline in both mental and physical health.

You can't enjoy traveling if you're not healthy and in reasonably good shape.

You need exercise to stay in good physical condition and you need to have good mental health; you need to keep active and have goals and dreams. It would help if you had something to look forward to every morning when you get up. (I'm talking about something other than getting to the coffee pot.)

To enjoy traveling, you have to be reasonably healthy.

For a lot of people, when they retire, they don't do much physical activity, they don't eat right, and they let their health go to pot. For others, their health wasn't that good to start with.

If you want to enjoy traveling, take steps now to get healthy. Have you had a physical lately? Are your blood pressure, blood sugar, and weight under control? These are three important health factors that you can control with diet, exercise, and medication.

If you're serious about wanting to travel and enjoy the experience, get a physical exam and get on a strict regimen to get these factors (and anything else that needs attention) under control.

By the way, if you smoke, you need to do whatever it takes to give up smoking. I know it's not easy, but there are medications that make it way easier than it used to be.

Don't kid yourself. If you're not going to give up smoking, there's nothing you can do that will keep you healthy for much longer.

The degree to which you maintain your physical and mental fitness after retirement will determine how much you will enjoy traveling.

To get in good physical shape and stay in shape, you need to find an activity you enjoy. If you hate every minute of a workout, you're not going to stick with it.

I don't like walking on a treadmill. It's the most boring exercise I can think of. I love to hike and run. I didn't run my first marathon until after I turned 60.

I like hiking up mountains to waterfalls. I like walking on a beach too, but walking on a beach doesn't seem like hiking.

What is the difference between walking and hiking? The Urban Dictionary describes it this way. When you're hiking, you can stop and pee, but when you're walking, you can't. There's no place. I think of walking on a beach or walking on a sidewalk and the definition is right. There's no place to stop and pee like there is if you're hiking on a mountain trail.

With my hiking, walking, and running, I get my heart rate up and build my leg muscles, but my upper body doesn't get much of a workout.

About the heaviest thing I lift daily is a coffee cup, but it's a coffee mug, so it's heavier than a regular cup of coffee.

Many people spend considerable time and effort to make sure they don't run out of money after they retire, but many don't pay enough attention to the fact that they may run out of health.

If you're going to travel, you're going to need health and money.

Maybe when you were working, you didn't have a lot of time for exercise and taking care of your health, but now that you're retired (or getting ready to retire) you can make exercise and taking care of your health a top priority.

Without your health, nothing else matters much.

Stress can kill you

One last point. One of the most significant things that affects your health is stress. Stress raises your blood pressure and reduces the effectiveness of your immune system. In my opinion, stress causes more health problems than any other factor.

The good news is that you have complete control over stress. Some people stay uptight and are always stressed out about something. The sad news is that being stressed out does not solve any of their problems, but it is killing them. Don't let this happen to you.

Exercise

Exercise is essential for good health, and good health is necessary if you're going to enjoy traveling.

Some people say that exercise is boring, but my thoughts are that if you think exercise is boring, try living in a nursing home.

I've heard it said that you can live without exercise and you can—you just can't live as long.

The benefits of regular exercise are overwhelming. You don't need to be convinced of that. You already know that. You just need to be motivated to do something about it.

It's essential to exercise your mind

A lot of people overlook the fact that you must exercise your mind. The phrase "Use it or lose it" applies to your mind as well as to your muscles.

It's essential to be using your mind and always be learning something new. You can learn a new language, learn to paint, learn Morse code, learn to play a musical instrument; anything that challenges your mind will help you stay sane.

Medications

When you're traveling for more than a week or two, you'll have to have a plan for your medications.

If you're traveling in the US, have your prescriptions filled at Walmart, CVS, or some other national chain. Their computers are all connected, and you can walk into any store in the chain and get your prescriptions refilled.

If you're going to be outside of the US, you can discuss this with your local pharmacist and he can put in a request with your insurance company to give you several weeks of medication. It's called "vacation mode."

There's a plan C. Except for narcotics, in most countries you can get medications without a prescription. It will probably be a different brand than you're used to, and the pills will look different, but it's the same medication.

When I'm traveling, I put my medications in Ziploc bags instead of the bottles they come in because they take up a lot less space that way.

I take the label off of the bottle and put it inside of the bag. That way there's no doubt about what's in the bag.

Obesity is widespread

That statement is true in more ways than one.

I've heard it said that women who carry a little extra weight tend to live longer than the men who say something about it. I don't doubt that for a minute.

Get enough sleep

When we're traveling, it's human nature to want to see everything and do everything; this is especially true if you're only going to be somewhere for a short amount of time. How do you find the time to do everything? The obvious way for a lot of inexperienced travelers is not to spend so much time sleeping.

Maybe you can get away with this for a day or two, but it's going to catch up with you. When you don't get enough sleep, you're not as mentally sharp and you won't have the stamina you usually have. Also, a lack of sleep will compromise your immune system. That's why a lot of people get sick when they travel.

Keep in mind that, just because you spend enough time in bed, you're not in your usual bed and you may not sleep as well or go to sleep as fast. Whatever it takes, get plenty of sleep when you're traveling.

Bottom line: Diet, exercise, and attitude are the three most important factors for staying healthy. The good news is that you have complete control over all three of these factors. I hope this chapter has convinced you to take control of your health so you can live and enjoy traveling for a long time. You can. It's your choice.

Chapter 16

Carve Your Plans in Jell-O

"Any idiot can face a crisis—it's day-to-day living that wears you out."

~ Anton Chekhov

When you're traveling, you will always be asking yourself, "Is this what I signed up for?" If you're not having fun and don't like what you're doing, change your mind and do something else.

Nobody wants people to think they're wishy-washy or that they can't make up their minds.

I say the heck with what people think. At this stage in your life you don't have to be logical, rational, or meet society's expectations. After all, you do have a firm plan. Remember that your plan is to travel and be happy.

How you accomplish that may (and should) change from time to time. There are certain trips that you can't know if you will like them or not until you take them.

So there's nothing wrong with planning a trip or going on a trip and then deciding that you don't like it. Or maybe you decided that it was fun for a while but now you want to do something else.

That's part of being free. You're free to change your mind.

I can still hear my grandmother saying, "Finish what you start." We've had that philosophy pounded into us all our lives, but now we don't have time left to finish everything we want to try.

We need a different strategy. Besides, my grandmother is gone, so she will never know that I changed my mind a lot and didn't finish everything I started. If I always go with her philosophy, maybe I should say that there's half of a chocolate cake in the refrigerator, perhaps I should finish that.

Start with an attitude of "I'm going to give this a try." As soon as you decide you've had enough of something, quit and do something else. Don't waste one of your precious minutes doing something after you've decided it's not what you want to do.

I'm retired. My plans are carved in Jell-O

Your motto should now be, "I'm retired. My plans are carved in Jell-O." Don't be ashamed of it. Be proud of the fact that you are now free enough to change your mind on a whim.

It's okay to have shaky plans

In my opinion, it's even desirable. There are so many places to travel and experience and so many enjoyable things to do. At this stage in your life, don't worry about what other people say and don't continue doing anything that's not bringing you joy. Follow Dr. Seuss's advice as he stated in the following quote:

"Be who you are and say what you feel because those who mind don't matter, and those who matter don't mind."

~ Dr. Seuss

Don't play it safe all the time—take some risks.

You don't want to play it safe all the time. You want to take some risks and then quickly change course when you see that something is not working out the way you thought it would.

Several major companies give annual awards for the worst ideas or the biggest failures of the year. By showing employees that it's okay to fail, they encourage risk-taking.

If you try a lot of new ideas and innovative options for things to do, places to go, and ways to live, you're going to experience what some people might call failures.

Keep this quote in mind as you try different lifestyles.

"Life does not get better by chance; it gets better by change."

~ Jim Rohn

Don't look at changing your mind about something as a failure. Give yourself an award for recognizing that what you're doing is not what you want to do, and then move on.

As soon as you decide to make a change in your plans, go out and reward yourself with a great dinner or splurge on a nice bottle of wine (or both). In some way, celebrate the fact that you're closer to finding out what you want to do and where you want to go. Then, of course, make a change.

There's no one right way to travel. It depends on your goals, desires, and situation. More than likely, after reading this book, the way you will travel will be different from most people's idea of traveling.

That's fine. Let them keep going on expensive (and boring) trips (**if** they ever get around to traveling at all) while you stick with your enjoyable, adventurous, low-cost (and maybe unorthodox) methods of traveling and having the time of your life while spending less money than it would cost you to stay home and not travel.

Bottom line: Be proud of the fact that your plans are carved in Jell-O and therefore they're shaky.

Chapter 17

Make Your First Trip Happen

"Don't stay away from church because there are so many hypocrites. There's always room for one more."

~ An unknown wise soul

I know this will not be your first trip. You've been traveling all your life, but this will be your first trip where you're traveling in a totally different way.

You're not going to be driving or flying somewhere and staying in a Holiday Inn or with relatives. That's not a trip. You've done that many times before and it's not much fun.

You've found a new way to travel where you don't spend much money; you relax and have a different and enjoyable experience.

You're a vagabond traveler—wandering from place to place with no real home. Okay, maybe you do still have your home, but you may soon be wondering why.

If you're going to do a lot of traveling, keeping your home is a significant expense that will greatly limit the amount of money you have for traveling.

I can understand you wanting to keep your home to start with, but seriously consider getting rid of your home or renting it if you're going to travel full-time.

Having to make a rent or mortgage payment, plus the other expenses of having a home, could almost double your monthly expenses.

If you're not going to be traveling more or less full-time, you might want to consider keeping your home, but let's talk about some options.

Your biggest travel expenses

One of the most significant traveling expenses is the costs you're still paying back home—mortgage, insurance, utilities, lawn care, maintenance, cable TV, Internet, etc.

These expenses can add up to more than your travel expenses.

Face the facts. You can't keep paying all of these expenses and travel on your Social Security income. You can travel and cover all of your costs with your Social Security income, but you can't cover your travel expenses plus still pay all of the costs back home. Be realistic. Something has to give.

If you're going to be traveling more or less full-time, the answer is simple. Get rid of your house (or rent it out). Even if your house is paid for, it's still an expensive burden.

The dilemma comes when you only want to travel part of the time.

Here are some options for part-time travel

House swapping—Like everything else in the world, there's a website for that:
https://www.homeexchange.com/

They have 400,000 homes available in 187 countries. You can find a home anywhere in the world. There's a $150 annual fee to be a member and you get unlimited exchanges.

I know the question you're dying to ask. "What if I find a house where I want to stay but that person is not interested in staying in my house?" You can offer them "Guest Points" that they can use later to stay in another member's house.

If someone wants to use the Guest Points to come to stay in your house when you're not traveling, no problem; your home is only available when you say it is. Also, it's an excellent opportunity for you to go visit your kids and spend time with the grandkids so you can free up your house. It's your choice.

Making your first trip happen

If you're going to be serious about traveling, make your first trip a month-long trip. Don't take off somewhere for a long weekend and call that traveling. You've done that before. Whether you travel internationally or stay in the US, get out and go somewhere. And then stay there and explore the area. There's a coffee shop down the street and a bookstore around the corner. There's more to see than just the cannon in the park downtown.

Follow the techniques I've described and book a place for a month, or maybe book two locations for two weeks each. This will be a little more expensive than booking one place for a month, but if you don't think you would be happy in one place for a month, booking two locations is an option. I like to stay in one place for a month or more—but to each his own.

House-Sitting is another option. You'll essentially be staying in someone's house and taking care of it while they're gone on vacation (or wherever).

It's a lot like house swapping, except no one comes to stay at your house. You'll still have all of your expenses back home, but at least you won't have to pay anything for a place to stay. The places you will be staying are usually nice houses. You'll be able to check them out online and see pictures before you agree to the deal.

You'll be watering plants, maybe taking care of pets, getting the mail, possibly receiving packages, etc. Everything you would normally do if you were living in the house.

There are several online websites to help you find a house in the place you want to visit. Below is a list.

https://www.housecarers.com/

https://www.mindmyhouse.com/index.php/

Nomador.com

Rover.com

SeniorsHomeExchange.com (membership is $65 for a three-year listing)

My favorite is HouseCarers.com because they will automatically send you notifications when a new listing posts in the area and date range you're interested in, and I've heard some really good things about them.

You can browse the house-sitting opportunities around the world without being a member, but you'll have to join and pay a membership fee to contact the homeowner and arrange things.

Depending on the website, the membership fees range from $20 to $50 a year.

A lot of the people applying to do house-sitting are young people, but most homeowners prefer retired, dependable, and somewhat handy house-sitters, and since that probably describes you you'll have a better chance of getting approved for the gig, but you have to apply early. The good deals are snapped up fast.

Bottom line: Do a reasonable amount of research, soul-searching, and fact-finding and then make your decision. You will never have all the information, but remember that it's easy to change your mind when you're living your new lifestyle. Remember, your plans are carved in Jell-O.

The important things are to have a dream and make a decision.

Remember,

"Most people who died yesterday had plans for today."

~ Unknown

Chapter 18

Closing Thoughts

"It's tough to make predictions, especially about the future."

~ Yogi Berra

It's not as hard to plan your leap into traveling when you don't think about it as planning how and where you want to live and travel long-term but rather what trip you want to try first.

This chapter is short because there's not much involved in planning your decision to travel. Do some research, think about your options, and then make your plan.

Implementing the plan is another story. That could take some time, but coming up with your plan shouldn't take long at all. Just remember it's a tentative plan and you're free to change it at any time (and you probably will). It's a lot easier and quicker to make a tentative plan than a permanent plan.

Trying something out as a potential retirement lifestyle is not like taking a job in Kansas and moving the family across the country. If you do that, you're stuck there, at least for a while.

Now that you're retired, you can move to Panama (or to Thailand) in a heartbeat and then come back or go somewhere else if you find that you don't like where you are.

Trying different lifestyles and living in other countries or different states can be part of the adventure.

By all means, when you're planning your leap into retirement, keep in mind that deciding to live in two (or more) places is a very viable and reasonable option. That's what I do. I spend a lot of time in more than two locations.

If you can, do most of your planning before you retire. You'll be a lot more relaxed then. Of course, your retirement might drop out of the sky when your company announces you're being downsized.

Take that as a big blessing. If you're downsized, you'll probably get a severance package. That's even better than just quitting.

One thing that's kind of like traveling is moving to a different town or even a foreign country. When a lot of people retire, they find they yearn for a change of scenery, new experiences, or a change of circumstances.

Living in a different place can feel like traveling, at least for a long time it can. There will be so many new things to see and do and new people to meet. The statement below describes how a lot of people feel about where they live.

"I have just returned from Boston. It is the only thing to do if you find yourself there."

~ Fred Allen

If this describes how you feel about where you're living, by all means start making plans to live someplace else. Rent a place and live there for six months to a year. If you don't like it, try somewhere else.

Even if you do like it, you might decide you want to live somewhere else for a while.

I don't think any place is perfect. I like to stay in one place for two or three months and then live somewhere else.

The way I do it is that I have a motorhome. I live in it for six or seven months, moving two or three times during that time. I like to live in the North Carolina mountains in the summer. It's cool up at 4,000 feet. I like to live by the beach in Florida or Texas in the winter months.

I like to travel internationally for five or six months. I pay $30 a month to store my motorhome and I cancel the collision insurance, so I have almost no expenses back in the US when traveling internationally.

I like to live where the temperature is always in the mid-70s. All I've worn for the last year is shorts and tee shirts, and unless somebody in the family gets married or dies, I probably won't wear long pants, a long-sleeve shirt, or a jacket this coming year either.

Some miscellaneous advice

Have an emergency fund. Travel on your Social Security, and travel like you were flat broke, but have access to a few thousand dollars all the time.

Whether it's a line of credit on a credit card or a separate bank account, don't carry the money with you.

It's a good idea to have a few hundred dollars in a secret place with you, but not the few thousand I'm talking about here.

Don't keep all your cash and all your credit cards in one place. Have a credit card and some cash with you and, if it's safe, keep a credit card and some cash in your room in a place where it can't be found in a hurry.

There's always the rare possibility that you could lose your wallet or have your bank account hacked.

Let the fun begin

If there were no unknowns, there wouldn't be any adventure. So, embrace the idea that unexpected good things and unexpected bad things are going to happen. Enjoy the adventure.

Spend a relaxing morning or afternoon sitting in a park and reading a book. You'll find it to be a wonderful experience. You'll enjoy the people you'll meet, the conversations you'll overhear, and the general feel for the area. You'll meet both locals and travelers. You'll find them all interesting.

Bottom line: You've worked hard and for many years, and now you're entitled to your monthly Social Security income.

You're ready to retire and do some traveling. Don't overanalyze the situation. Just simplify, make a decision, and go. Whether you plan to travel in the US or do some international traveling it doesn't matter—just go. Stay a week, a month, or a year and then go somewhere else.

You're free as a bird. Enjoy your new traveling lifestyle, and with the help of the information in this book, you now know how to travel on just your Social Security income.

Did You Like This Book?

If you liked this book, I need your help.

I would appreciate it if you would take a minute and leave a review on Amazon. (You can do it in only one minute.)

Writing a review is not like writing a high school book report. All you need to do is write a sentence or two saying that you liked the book.

Thank you,

Jerry Minchey

P.S. On the following pages are some of my other books that you might find interesting and entertaining.

(You can find them on Amazon.)

Other books by the author available on Amazon

More books by the author available on Amazon

Made in the USA
Coppell, TX
10 February 2026

71749128R00089